Scriptures of Mercy
The Love of God in the Old Testament

by
Fr Adrian Graffy

All booklets are published thanks to the generous support of the members of the Catholic Truth Society

CATHOLIC TRUTH SOCIETY
PUBLISHERS TO THE HOLY SEE

Contents

Introduction 3
In the Beginning - the Mercy of God 4
Esau Embraces his Brother Jacob 8
Joseph Pardons his Brothers 12
God Sets the People Free 16
God the Merciful 20
David Pleads for Forgiveness.................... 24
The Parental Compassion of God................. 28
A Call to Repentance 32
Jonah Struggles with God's Mercy 36
The Eternal Covenant of God's Mercy 40
Remember the Mercy of God 44
God, Lover of Life............................ 48

First published 2016 by The Incorporated Catholic Truth Society 40-46 Harleyford Road London SE11 5AY Tel: 020 7640 0042 Fax: 020 7640 0046. Copyright 2016 © Adrian Graffy. This edition © 2016 The Incorporated Catholic Truth Society.
ISBN 978 1 78469 128 8

The Bible quotations in this booklet are taken from
The New Jerusalem Bible.

Introduction

The story of the Bible is the story of God's mercy. This mercy is shown in the actions of God towards the creation, and towards human beings in particular. This mercy is apparent from the beginning, as God demonstrates loving care, and it is often seen in the way human beings act towards each other. The God of compassion calls us to compassion.

The texts are explained in such a way that anyone can access them. This booklet should help anyone who has been misled by the common mistake that the God of the Old Testament is a God of cruelty and punishment. Christians of course will be able to see that these texts prepare for the revelation brought by Christ, that God is love.

The twelve readings in this booklet provide a wide variety of Old Testament passages which speak of God's mercy, and the way this mercy is lived out by human beings. There are many other texts which might have been included. God's mercy begins from the very beginning, and, as Psalm 136 (135) says, "it endures for ever".

Bible texts are quoted from the *Jerusalem Bible*, with small adjustments in line with the original languages. The passage from Psalm 51 (50) is taken from the *Grail Psalter*.

1

In the Beginning - the Mercy of God

GENESIS 3:8-13, 20-21, 23

The man and his wife heard the sound of the Lord God walking in the garden in the cool of the day, and they hid from the Lord God among the trees of the garden. But the Lord God called to the man. "Where are you?" he asked. "I heard the sound of you in the garden," he replied. "I was afraid because I was naked, so I hid." "Who told you that you were naked?" he asked. "Have you been eating of the tree I forbade you to eat?" The man replied, "It was the woman you put with me, she gave me the fruit, and I ate it." Then the Lord God asked the woman, "What is this you have done?" The woman replied, "The serpent tempted me and I ate."

The man named his wife "Eve" because she was the mother of all those who live. The Lord God made clothes out of skins for the man and his wife, and they put them on. So the Lord God expelled the man from the garden of Eden, to till the soil from which he had been taken.

In the Beginning - the Mercy of God

The opening chapters of the Book of Genesis, the first book of the Bible, are unique. They address fundamental questions. Through these ancient stories we learn about the goodness of God, the beauty of God's creation, the place of human beings in it, and so much more. After two stories about God bringing the creation into existence, the man and his wife are in a garden. Everything is provided for their needs. Furthermore, they are given the uniquely human gift of free choice. The story teaches us that human beings can make the wrong choices, that we can choose what is not good, and that such choices have consequences.

When we choose what is not good, we place distance between ourselves and God, and between ourselves and others. The garden of God is lost, and the trust between the man and the woman is undermined as each of them passes the buck, the man to the woman and the woman to the serpent in a blaming game.

Despite all this the mercy of God endures. The justice of God, unlike human justice, embraces mercy. That God makes clothes for the man and his wife teaches us that God continues to be concerned about the safety and the dignity of human beings. God's disappointment at the wrong choices we make does not stop God from loving us. This is the central message of mercy, and it is found throughout the Bible, from the very start, to the very end.

> • Can you see how the story of God making clothes points to a deeper and enduring truth about God?
>
> • Consider your wrong choices and how the mercy of God was available in spite of them.

2

Esau Embraces his Brother Jacob

GENESIS 33:1-4, 8-11

Looking up, Jacob saw Esau arriving with four hundred men. Accordingly he divided the children between Leah, Rachel and the two slave girls. He put the slave girls and their children in front, with Leah and her children following, and Rachel and Joseph behind. He himself went ahead of them and bowed to the ground seven times before going up to his brother. But Esau ran to meet him, took him in his arms and held him close, and wept.

Esau asked, "What was the meaning of all the company that I have met?" "It is to win my lord's favour," Jacob replied. "Brother, I have plenty," Esau answered, "keep what is yours." Jacob insisted, "Please, if I have found favour with you, accept the gift I offer. To speak truly, I came into your presence as into the presence of God, but you have received me kindly. So accept the gift I have brought for you; since God has been generous to me, I have all I need." And he urged him, and Esau accepted.

Esau Embraces his Brother Jacob

God's mercy, which is displayed in the creation and in God's dealings with people, is to be seen also in the history of the chosen people. God's mercy is shown to Abraham, the father of the Jews, when God promises him land and numerous descendants, and undertakes to be with him on his nomadic journeys. God's mercy is seen especially in the birth of Abraham's son Isaac, and in due course to Isaac and his wife Rebekah are born the twin sons, Esau and Jacob.

Through the collusion and trickery of his mother, Jacob, who is the second born son, wins the blessing meant for the first born from his aged father. The seeds of enmity are thus sown between Jacob and Esau, so that Jacob, warned by his mother, leaves for a distant country where he makes his fortune.

Jacob returns to his homeland, with his wives and children and multitudes of flocks. As he approaches the land of Edom, the land of his brother Esau, Jacob sends gifts in an attempt to placate him and to heal the ill feeling between them. He is warned that Esau is arriving with four hundred men and is fearful of the encounter.

That night Jacob has a strange vision of wrestling with God's angel. In the morning he is ready to meet his brother. Jacob bows seven times as he approaches Esau, but Esau rushes towards him and embraces him, weeping. The God of mercy invites us to be merciful. Sometimes mercy comes from an unexpected source.

• How often have you experienced goodness coming from an unexpected source?

• Is there anyone you can surprise by offering them mercy, just as Esau did to Jacob?

3

Joseph Pardons his Brothers

GENESIS 50:15-21

Seeing that their father Jacob was dead, Joseph's brothers said, "What if Joseph intends to treat us as enemies and repay us in full for all the wrong we did him?" So they sent this message to Joseph: "Before your father died he gave us this order: 'You must say to Joseph: Forgive your brothers their crime and their sin and all the wrong they did you.' Now therefore, we beg you, forgive the crime of the servants of your father's God." Joseph wept at the message they sent to him.

His brothers came and fell down before him. "We present ourselves before you," they said, "as your slaves." But Joseph answered them, "Do not be afraid. Is it for me to put myself in God's place? The evil you planned to do me has by God's design been turned to good, that he might bring about, as indeed he has, the deliverance of a numerous people. So you need not be afraid. I myself will provide for you and your dependants." In this way he reassured them with words that touched their hearts.

Joseph Pardons his Brothers

As the story of the chosen people continues we are faced with another family crisis. Jacob has a favourite son called Joseph, son of his beloved wife Rachel, and he loves Joseph more than all his other sons. This Joseph is the recipient of the amazing coat with long sleeves. His brothers are jealous and kidnap Joseph, selling him into slavery in Egypt. When famine hits Canaan their homeland, the brothers go to Egypt to beg for food. They encounter a powerful government official who has charge of the food stores. He treats them with kindness. This official is none other than Joseph.

Joseph does not reveal his true identity, but tests his brothers to see if they truly regret their actions. In a moving scene Joseph finally reveals himself as their brother.

Their father Jacob also makes the journey to Egypt, and he dies there. Understandably the brothers fear that Joseph will now repay them for the evil done to him years earlier. Their approach to Joseph comes first of all in a message, and then face to face. On both occasions we are aware of the power of words to heal and to touch hearts.

Joseph chooses to forgive rather than punish. Like Esau, who chose to forgive his brother rather than take revenge, Joseph assures his brothers that they have nothing to fear. He explains that God is capable of drawing good out of evil. But God cannot achieve this good purpose without the willingness of Joseph to forgive the evil done to him. The brothers sought to ruin Joseph's life, but Joseph survives to save their lives in time of need.

• Does it surprise you that God can draw good out of evil?

• Have you ever behaved like Joseph, offering the forgiveness that mercy suggests, rather than demanding punishment?

4

God Sets the People Free

EXODUS 3:4-8

The Lord saw Moses go forward to look, and God called to him from the middle of the bush. "Moses, Moses," he said. "Here I am," he answered. "Come no nearer," he said. "Take off your shoes, for the place on which you stand is holy ground. I am the God of your father," he said, "the God of Abraham, the God of Isaac, and the God of Jacob." At this Moses covered his face, afraid to look at God.

And the Lord said, "I have seen the miserable state of my people in Egypt. I have heard their appeal to be free of their slave-drivers. Yes, I am well aware of their suffering. I mean to deliver them out of the hands of the Egyptians and bring them up out of that land to a land rich and broad, a land where milk and honey flow."

God Sets the People Free

After the death of Jacob and his sons the people remain in Egypt, but a new Pharaoh, who does not know Joseph, enslaves them, and the next chapter in the history of the people of God begins. The God of mercy is aware of the plight of the people, and appears to Moses in the strange spectacle of the burning bush. This is the God worshipped by the first leaders of the people, by Abraham, Isaac and Jacob. Moses, born of a Jewish mother, but brought up in the Egyptian court, recognises the holiness of God, and covers his face in God's presence.

The story of the exodus, the escape of the people from slavery in Egypt, is the fundamental story of liberation. It proclaims that God is a God of freedom, who desires freedom for all people. The exodus is celebrated still among the Jews at the great feast of Passover. It has a universal significance.

The passage speaks of God's awareness of the misery of the people. God will use Moses to bring them to freedom. God invites people to work for freedom and for justice and peace among all the peoples of the world. God cannot achieve these aims without assistance.

Despite his privileged access to God, Moses is reluctant to take on the task, and, as the story progresses, offers no fewer than five objections, which God dismisses one by one. The mercy of God needs collaborators, and can be very persuasive when human beings are slow to respond to God's call. The land of milk and honey, where the riches of the earth are freely available to all, is promised.

• What can you do today to liberate others, and to make the mercy of God real for them?

• Think of an act of mercy you have repeatedly put off, and resolve to postpone it no longer.

5

God the Merciful

EXODUS 34:6-9

Moses called on the name of the Lord. The Lord passed before him and proclaimed, "The Lord, the Lord, a God of tenderness and compassion, slow to anger, rich in kindness and faithfulness; for thousands he maintains his kindness, forgives faults, transgressions, sin; yet he lets nothing go unchecked, punishing the father's fault in the sons and in the grandsons to the third and fourth generation." And Moses bowed down to the ground at once and worshipped. "If I have indeed won your favour, Lord," he said, "let my Lord come with us, I beg. True, they are a headstrong people, but forgive us our faults and our sins, and adopt us as your heritage."

God the Merciful

The book of Exodus recounts how, after a series of plagues, Pharaoh lets the people go. The dramatic crossing of the Red Sea underlines God's commitment and determination to liberate the people. Moses leads them to Mount Sinai, and on the mountain he receives the law from God. These are the foundation events for the Hebrew nation. And yet the people turn away from God, and have a golden calf made for worship, so that Moses must intercede for them before God.

Moses desires to know more of God, and even to see the glory of God. God's response is given in the speech, which lists God's attributes. The Lord is merciful and compassionate, slow to anger and rich in kindness and faithfulness. The Hebrew word translated as 'kindness' is *hesed*, a very rich and powerful concept which stands for the faithful covenant love of God. God maintains this faithful love for a thousand generations, forgiving faults and sins. Punishment, on the other hand, can only reach the fourth generation, and would only apply to those who have followed the evil ways of their ancestors.

Moses pleads for the people, trusting that God's mercy will win the day. When these words of God are quoted in later scripture, as we shall see, the reference to continuing punishment is omitted. The mercy of God opens up new possibilities. Despite sin, Moses insists that God should remain faithful to his heritage. The people are admittedly headstrong, says Moses, but God should not let this be an obstacle to showing mercy. The whole emphasis of the exchange is positive. While sin and failure are acknowledged, the faithful love of God is given far greater emphasis.

The covenant can be renewed for God is merciful, the desert wanderings are resumed and God will lead the Israelites to the promised land.

- God is determined to show mercy in spite of human sin. Have your actions ever imitated God's preference for mercy?

- What does the faithful love of God mean to you?

6

David Pleads for Forgiveness

PSALM 51 (50): 3-6, 8-12

Have mercy on me, God, in your kindness;
in your compassion blot out my offence.

O wash me more and more from my guilt,
and cleanse me from my sin.

My offences truly I know them;
my sin is always before me.

Against you, you alone, have I sinned;
what is evil in your sight I have done.

Indeed you love truth in the heart;
then in the secret of my heart teach me wisdom.

O purify me, then I shall be clean;
O wash me, I shall be whiter than snow.

Make me hear rejoicing and gladness,
that the bones you have crushed may thrill.

From my sins turn away your face,
and blot out all my guilt.

A pure heart create for me, O God,
put a steadfast spirit within me.

David Pleads for Forgiveness

Settled in the promised land, the people choose Saul as their first king. His reign ends in tragedy. The prospects for David look far brighter. He unites the tribes of Israel, establishing Jerusalem as his capital, and even considers building a temple for God.

But David is also remembered for his sins. When the army is away at war he takes for himself the wife of a faithful army officer, Uriah the Hittite. Bathsheba becomes pregnant. Adultery is David's first crime. He plots to have Uriah brought back from the war, pressurising him to go to his house and sleep with his wife. Uriah's sense of solidarity with his companions at war means that he does not go to his house. On his return to the battle David sends instructions that Uriah be placed in the thick of the battle and abandoned there so that he is killed. David's second crime is murder.

Psalm 51, known as 50 in some texts, is presented as the prayer of David at this time. The psalm pleads for mercy. Instinctively David recalls those qualities of God revealed to Moses. In spite of his sins David recalls the kindness, the *hesed* of God, and God's compassion. There is a heavy emphasis on the need to be cleansed. "Wash me from my guilt, and cleanse me from my sin," he prays. The psalm displays a rich vocabulary of sin, using many different words so that the enormity of David's sins is truly recognised. David's behaviour will have far reaching consequences for his family.

Yet the mercy of God is stronger, and David is granted forgiveness. The psalm shows a foretaste of this as David prays "make me hear rejoicing and gladness". He trusts that God can create for him a pure heart and a steadfast spirit.

• God shows mercy and compassion to the sinner who acknowledges his guilt. Recall the times when you have received forgiveness after admitting your fault.

• Actions have consequences, but God's love is stronger. Trust that God can create a new heart for those who seek it.

7

The Parental Compassion of God

HOSEA 11:1-4, 8-9

When Israel was a child, I loved him, and I called my son out of Egypt. But the more I called to them, the further they went from me; they have offered sacrifice to the Baals and set their offerings smoking before the idols. I myself taught Ephraim to walk, I took them in my arms; yet they have not understood that I was the one looking after them. I led them with reins of kindness, with leading strings of love. I was like someone who lifts an infant close against his cheek; stooping down to him I gave him his food.

Ephraim, how could I part with you? Israel, how could I give you up? How could I treat you like Admah, or deal with you like Zeboiim? My heart recoils from it, my whole being trembles at the thought. I will not give rein to my fierce anger, I will not destroy Ephraim again, for I am God, not man: I am the Holy One in your midst and have no wish to destroy.

The Parental Compassion of God

It is the role of the prophet to speak for God, to bring God's words to the people. Hosea spoke to the northern tribes of Israel, telling them that God's love was constant despite their infidelity. The prophet had been the victim of infidelity himself, which gave him a profound insight into God's love. Just as Hosea continued to be faithful to an unfaithful wife, so God maintained fidelity to unfaithful Israel.

The passage we have read speaks of God as the parent who has loved Israel since the beginning. That love was demonstrated above all in the exodus from Egypt, but Israel's response was to turn away from God. In infidelity Israel pursues the "Baals", the local gods of nature, and resorts to idols. Despite the loving care shown by God in bringing up "Ephraim", another name for Israel, they have not acknowledged that God is the source of their well being.

Hosea, drawing no doubt on his own experience, speaks of the turmoil of God's emotions. God's love is so intense that God cannot destroy Israel. He speaks of Admah and Zeboiim, cities in the area of Sodom and Gomorrah, places destroyed by fire and brimstone. God could not possibly treat Israel in this way.

God's heart is not able to bring about such destruction. The reason given is that God is "God, not man". The will of God is not man's destruction, no matter how man behaves, but a relationship of self-giving love, as God is compared to a lover, and to a parent desperate for the well-being of a dearly-loved child.

• Does it help to consider the love of God in the light of human emotions?

• Do these words of an ancient prophet still give us insight into the mercy of God?

8

A Call to Repentance

JOEL 2:12-14, 17-18

But now - it is the Lord who speaks - come back to me with all your heart, fasting, weeping, mourning. Let your hearts be broken, not your garments torn, turn to the Lord your God again, for he is all tenderness and compassion, slow to anger, rich in graciousness, and ready to relent. Who knows if he will not turn again, will not relent, will not leave a blessing as he passes, oblation and libation for the Lord your God?

Between the vestibule and altar let the priests, the ministers of the Lord, lament. Let them say, "Spare your people, Lord! Do not make your heritage a thing of shame, a byword for the nations. Why should it be said among the nations, 'Where is their God?'"

Then the Lord, jealous on behalf of his land, took pity on the people.

A Call to Repentance

This passage from the book of the prophet Joel raises an important issue, an issue still with us today, a question raised repeatedly in human life. How should natural disasters be understood? Are they brought about by God as punishment, or are they simply part of the free working of the created world? The background to the prophet's words is a plague of locusts. Joel seems to understand this as a punishment for sin. Such an interpretation of natural disasters has not stood the test of time. The theology found here has been rethought, not least because many of the victims of disasters are clearly guiltless.

The call to repentance in this passage is nevertheless valid as an invitation to live better lives, and is used by Christians at the beginning of Lent. The invitation to return to the Lord is an invitation to change. It includes fasting and weeping and mourning, but the emphasis is on a change of heart. Such a return to God in repentance is encouraged by recalling the attributes of God made known to Moses. God is a God of "tenderness and compassion, slow to anger, rich in graciousness, and ready to relent". The traditional reference to God's punishment to the third and fourth generation is omitted and God is said to relent of evil. God will not inflict punishment, but will deliver a blessing. Once a good harvest is received, sacred offerings, "oblation and libation", will be made once more.

Israel is at this stage a nation among nations. There is a concern that the God of Israel should not be derided by foreigners as a powerless God.

• How are we to understand the natural disasters which God allows to happen?

• How concerned should we be about the reputation of our God, and of our faith?

9

Jonah Struggles with God's Mercy

JONAH 4:1-4, 11

Jonah was very indignant and he fell into a rage. He prayed to the Lord, and said, "Ah! Lord, is not this just as I said would happen when I was still at home? That was why I went and fled to Tarshish: I knew that you were a God of tenderness and compassion, slow to anger, rich in graciousness, relenting from evil. So now, Lord, please take away my life, for I might as well be dead as go on living." The Lord replied, "Are you right to be angry?"

The Lord said: "Am I not to feel sorry for Nineveh, the great city, in which there are more than a hundred and twenty thousand people who cannot tell their right hand from their left, to say nothing of all the animals?"

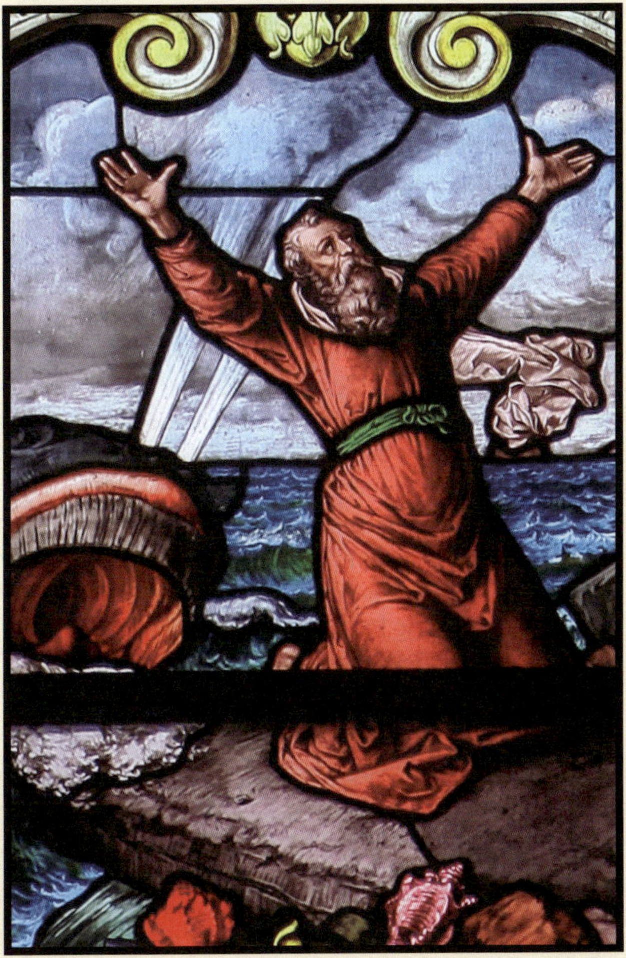

Jonah Struggles with God's Mercy

The book of Jonah, unlike other books of the prophets, does not contain a collection of the words Jonah preached, but is a story about Jonah the prophet, who really struggles with his vocation. Called to proclaim the mercy of God, he does his best to avoid the calling. He tries to get to Tarshish, a city in the furthest west, rather than travel east as God wishes. He does not agree that the mercy of God should extend to the people of Nineveh, capital of the Assyrian empire, for the Assyrians are the arch enemies of Israel. God, determined to get Jonah to Nineveh, even resorts to using a whale to achieve this.

The climax of the story comes when Jonah finally preaches the message to the people of Nineveh, and is disappointed, even angry, when God shows them mercy. Jonah, just like Joel, recalls the attributes of God announced to Moses. God is "a God of tenderness and compassion, slow to anger, rich in graciousness, relenting from evil." God is reluctant to inflict punishment. But Jonah does not think that God should be merciful, certainly not to the people of Nineveh.

Jonah is so upset about all this that he would rather die, and pleads with God to take his life. God teaches Jonah the lesson of mercy. Jonah's anger is a selfish anger. His heart is unable to reach out to others. The heart of God is different, God explains, and mercy should certainly extend to this great multitude of people "who cannot tell their right hand from their left". In other words, while Israel has had the privilege of God's word and God's revelation, other nations, who have not had this benefit, are still looked upon with mercy by God. The final phrase of the book opens up the argument to all creation, as God offers mercy even to the animals.

• Do you think there should be limits to the mercy of God? If so, what would they be?

• Can you recall a time you were angry that mercy had been shown to someone? Can you learn the lesson that Jonah could not learn?

10

The Eternal Covenant of God's Mercy

ISAIAH 54:6-10

Like a forsaken wife, distressed in spirit, the Lord calls you back. Does a man cast off the wife of his youth? says the Lord. I did forsake you for a brief moment, but with great mercy will I take you back. In excess of anger, for a moment I hid my face from you, but with everlasting love I have taken pity on you, says the Lord, your redeemer. I am now as I was in the days of Noah, when I swore that Noah's waters should never flood the world again. So now I swear concerning my anger with you and the threats I made against you: for the mountains may depart, the hills be shaken, but my love for you will never leave you, and my covenant of peace with you will never be shaken, says the Lord, who takes pity on you.

IN ARCHA SALVATUR NOE A DILUVIO

The Eternal Covenant of God's Mercy

The later chapters of the book of the prophet Isaiah contain the preaching of a prophet of the exile. Israel has lost everything, and is suffering deportation in the land of Babylon. The land, the monarchy, the temple, all are lost. But this prophet announces a new start, and, in a way similar to how Hosea spoke of God's relationship with Israel, this prophet too speaks of God taking back a forsaken wife. After a time of loss and sadness there is a new beginning.

God announces this new time as motivated by great mercy, and driven by everlasting love. God's love, God's kindness, the *hesed* made known to Moses, lasts for ever. The prophet considers the time of exile and loss as brought about by God's anger. Later theology would seek to avoid attributing disasters to the anger of God. God rather observes with compassion the tragedies and sufferings which human beings endure and often inflict on each other.

God's announces a new commitment sealed with an oath. The oath made to Noah, that the waters of the flood would never more cover the whole earth, is recalled as this new commitment of everlasting love is announced.

God also promises a covenant of peace. Throughout the history of the people of God covenants are made. The exile calls for a new covenant, which this prophet describes as "a covenant of peace". God's commitment to the people is more enduring than the mountains and the hills. All of this is brought about by the "Lord, who takes pity on you". God observes human life and the tragedies it brings, but never ceases to make mercy and love available for the whole of creation. God awaits our human response.

• Why does God allow so much suffering and tragedy in the world?

• Is God really a God of mercy, available at all times, and to all peoples?

11

Remember the Mercy of God

ECCLESIASTICUS 28:2-7

Forgive your neighbour the hurt he does you, and, when you pray, your sins will be forgiven. If someone nurses anger against another, can he then demand compassion from the Lord? Showing no pity for one like himself, can he then plead for his own sins? Mere creature of flesh, he cherishes resentment; who will forgive him his sins? Remember the last things, and stop hating. Remember dissolution and death, and live by the commandments. Remember the commandments, and do not bear your neighbour ill will. Remember the covenant of the Most High, and overlook the offence.

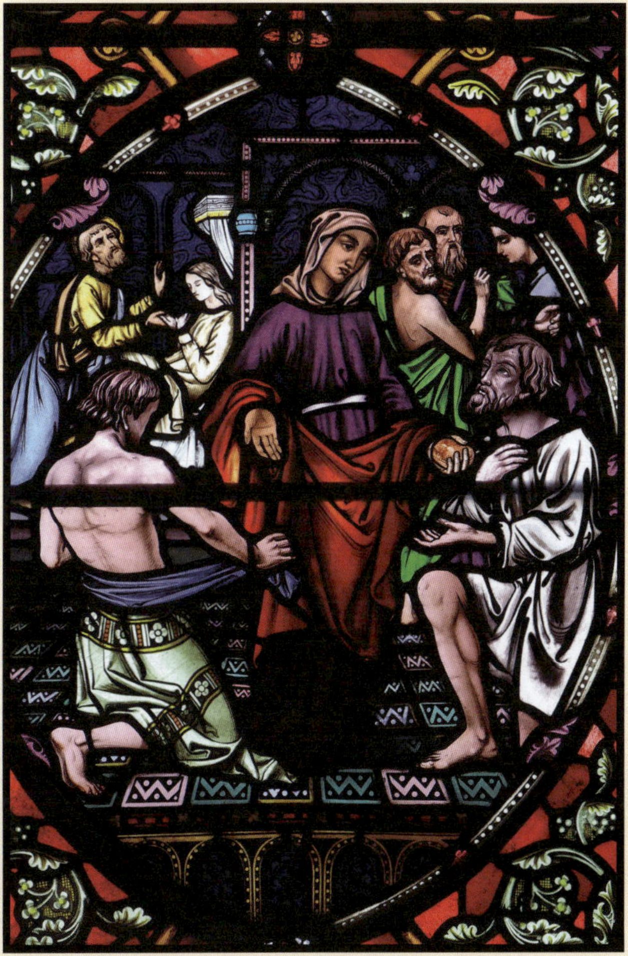

Remember the Mercy of God

We have seen how the mercy of God is present throughout the Scriptures, in the narrative books of the Old Testament and also in the prophets. The books often called the "wisdom literature", in which we find wide-ranging considerations of life, faith and the problems of living in the sight of God, also contain references to God's mercy, and to the living out of that mercy.

A wise teacher called Jesus, son of Sira, compiled a book of sayings in Jerusalem. It was his grandson, a member of the Jewish community in Egypt in the second century before Christ, who translated these sayings from Hebrew into Greek, the international language of the day. The book of the wisdom of the son of Sira is not found in the scriptures of the Hebrew Bible, but the Greek translation was accepted by early Christians, who would call the book Ecclesiasticus, the "book of the church". Early Christians treasured these wise sayings of a Jewish teacher and were determined to preserve them.

Whoever is familiar with the words of Jesus of Nazareth will recognise some similarities in the teaching of Jesus son of Sira. Our passage opens with words which recall the Lord's Prayer. The close connection between forgiving others and expecting to be forgiven by God is highlighted. Anger in the heart against a brother or sister is the wrong point of departure in pleading for God's compassion. This teaching is repeated throughout the first verses of our passage.

The passage continues with a repeated invitation to remembering. This writer's ideas about life after death are not entirely clear. He shares the Jewish belief in Sheol, the land of the dead, from where no one can praise God. God's mercy is available to those who turn to God in this life. The encouragement is to show mercy while we still can. In this way we maintain fidelity to the commandments of God and to the covenant of the God of mercy.

- Are you surprised that some of this passage is similar to the teaching of Jesus of Nazareth?

- How useful do you think it is to remember the deeper realities of life and faith?

12

God, Lover of Life

WISDOM 11:21-12:1

For your great strength is always at your call; who can withstand the might of your arm? In your sight the whole world is like a grain of dust that tips the scales, like a drop of morning dew falling on the ground. Yet you are merciful to all, because you can do all things, and overlook men's sins so that they can repent. Yes, you love all that exists, and you hold nothing of what you have made in abhorrence, for, had you hated anything, you would not have formed it. And how, had you not willed it, could a thing persist, how be conserved if not called forth by you? You spare all things, because all things are yours, Lord, lover of life, you whose imperishable spirit is in all.

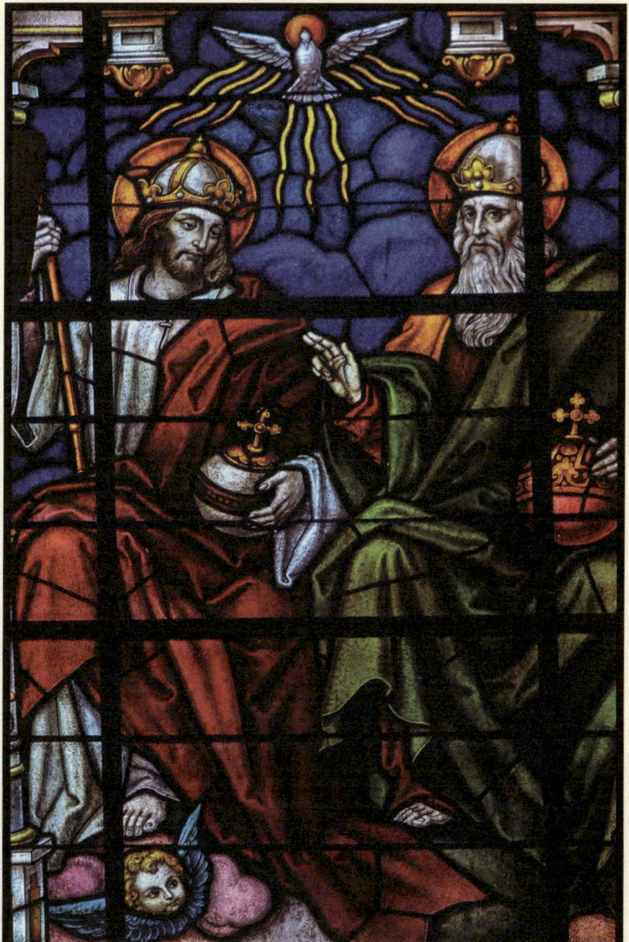

God, Lover of Life

Our final passage comes from what is probably the latest book in our Old Testament scriptures. It is known as the Wisdom of Solomon, but was not written by Solomon. In its title King Solomon and his wisdom are honoured, but this book was written many centuries later, probably in the first century before Christ, and produced by the Jewish community residing in Egypt at that time. It was written in Greek, the international language of the day. The writer composes prayers and reflections which he puts on the lips of Solomon. These words speak of the faith and hope of the Jews in Egypt, including the hope of immortality.

Towards the end of the book the author has been reflecting on the exodus from Egypt, the great act of mercy of God to Israel. This fundamental act of salvation still has meaning many centuries later. The writer considers how God showed mercy even to the Egyptians by not unleashing full power against them from the start.

From this the writer derives a principle of God's action. God's irresistible power is always available, yet God is merciful, merciful to all, leaving time for repentance. The mercy of God derives from God's love, the love that maintains everything in existence. God spares all things.

The writer gives God the extraordinary though quite natural title of "lover of life". Furthermore he speaks of God's imperishable spirit being present in all things. He has already asserted that the souls of the virtuous are in God's hands after death. The mercy of the God of life has no limit.

This very late book of the Old Testament confirms in its reflective way the deepest insights about the mercy of God displayed throughout the holy scriptures of the Old Testament. These insights are thoroughly confirmed and brought to fulfilment by Jesus Christ.

• Do you think "lover of life" is a helpful way to consider God?

• How challenging is it to hear that the imperishable spirit of God is in all things?

Picture credits

Page 5: Adam and Eve in the Garden of Eden, Brussels Cathedral © Jorisvo / Shutterstock.com

Page 9: Jacob, Notre Dame church, Dinant, Belgium © Jorisvo / Shutterstock.com

Page 13: Joseph, Notre Dame church, Dinant, Belgium © Jorisvo / Shutterstock.com

Page 17: Moses, Dom of Cologne, Germany © Jorisvo / Shutterstock.com

Page 21: Moses, © Howgill

Page 25: King David, Strasbourg Cathedral, France © Jorisvo / Shutterstock.com

Page 29: Samuel and Eli the priest, a detail of a window by Edward Burne-Jones in Christ Church Cathedral, Oxford. Courtesy of © Fr Lawrence Lew, OP

Page 33: The twenty-third psalm window in Grace Cathedral, by Connick Studios of Boston. Courtesy of © Fr Lawrence Lew, OP

Page 37: Jonah and the whale, Gamla Stan, Stockholm © Jorisvo / Shutterstock.com

Page 41: Noah's Ark, Ely Cathedral © Olan / Shutterstock.com

Page 45: Woman helping the poor © Howgill

Page 49: The Holy Trinity, Malaga Cathedral, Spain © Jorisvo / Shutterstock.com

Gospels of Mercy
12 Steps to the Love of God

Fr Adrian Graffy

Draw closer to God's mercy with this guide to the Gospels of Mercy. Adrian Graffy takes us on a step by step journey to discovering Christ's Mercy through the Scriptures. A selection of Gospels especially chosen for their theme of Mercy and which relate to Pope Francis' intentions for the Year of Mercy appears alongside a thoughtful meditation. Great reading for the Year of Mercy which will help us consider and practise this part of the Christian faith.

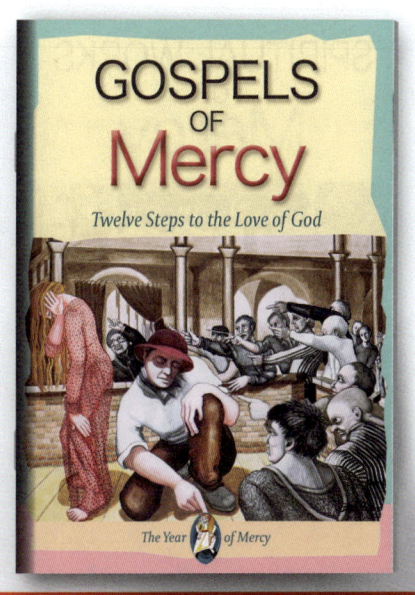

SC118   ISBN 978 1 78469 095 3

Spiritual Works of Mercy

Mgr Paul Grogan

Most Christians want to live an active faith yet feel perplexed about how to do so. The seven interconnected "spiritual works of mercy" come to our aid: counselling the doubtful; instructing the ignorant; admonishing sinners; comforting the afflicted; forgiving offences; bearing wrongs patiently; and praying for the living and the dead. Through such acts of mercy we can respond fully to God's goodness towards us, involving conversion of our interior life: such acts are truly God's acts of mercy; we, mere human agents for God to alleviate people's unhappiness.

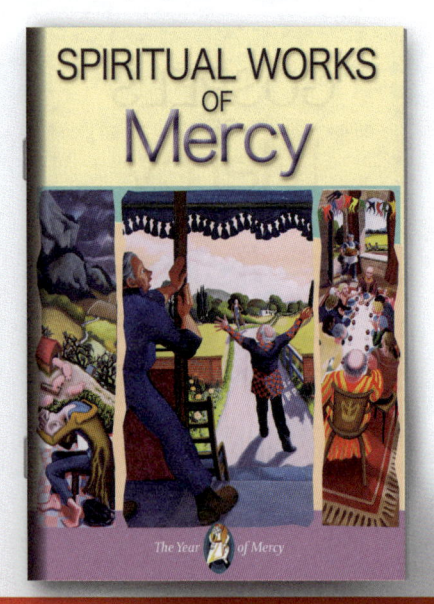

Corporal Works of Mercy
Mercy in Action

Mgr Richard Atherton

Feeding the hungry and thirsty, clothing the naked, housing the homeless, visiting the imprisoned, visiting the sick, and burying the dead - Pope Francis wants us to stop and think again, especially during the Year of Mercy. Are these things I can do, or are they for others to get on with? What good do they do? Actions of mercy are often terribly ordinary and doable. Mgr Atherton guides us through the spiritual and practical matters that Love asks of all Christians.

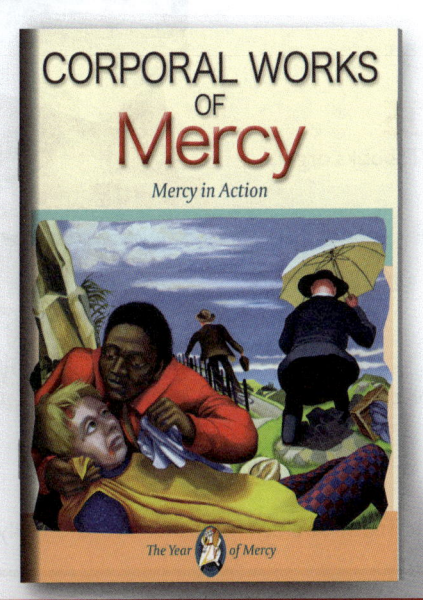

A world of Catholic reading at your fingertips...

Catholic Faith, Life & Truth for all

CTS
www.CTSbooks.org

twitter: @CTSpublishers

facebook.com/CTSpublishers

Catholic Truth Society, Publishers to the Holy See.